WHEN THE TIDE IS LOW

WHEN THE TIDE IS LOW

30 Days of Biblical Encouragement for Those Who Love the Ocean

April F. Cooper
With Contributions From: H. Davis Cooper

ELM HILL

A Division of
HarperCollins Christian Publishing

www.elmhillbooks.com

When the Tide Is Low
30 Days of Biblical Encouragement for Those Who Love the Ocean

Published in Nashville, Tennessee, by Elm Hill, an imprint of Thomas Nelson. Elm Hill and Thomas Nelson are registered trademarks of HarperCollins Christian Publishing, Inc.

Edited by Linda Zenns

Elm Hill titles may be purchased in bulk for educational, business, fund-raising, or sales promotional use. For information, please e-mail SpecialMarkets@ThomasNelson.com.

Library of Congress Cataloging-in-Publication Data

Library of Congress Control Number: 2018957012

ISBN 978-1-595558831 (Paperback)
ISBN 978-1-595558732 (eBook)

SPECIAL THANKS

To the man in my life who is after God's own heart,
my kind and loving husband, Davis Cooper,
and to my four personal gifts from above—my children:
Steven, Aiden, Leila, and Bella.

"Thy word is a lamp unto my feet, and a light unto my path."

(PSALM 119:105 KJV)

FOREWORD

As I walk along the shore, I cannot help but reflect on God's grace, beauty, and majesty. The waves are repetitive but unique in size, formation, speed, and sound. Every drop of water in the waves has worked together to visibly take the shape of what we see as a rolling tide. In our lives, God's grace, beauty, and majesty work the exact same way. Our daily lives may seem repetitive with the alarm clock and the same routines day in and day out, but every minute of our lives have worked together to visibly shape what we call our own walk. The hardest of these minutes often comes when there is a struggle, a crisis, or sadness with which we must personally deal or with which we help someone else to deal. Those are the days when the ocean is roaring, the waves are rough, and the wind is strong. Those are the days when it seems our ships are seemingly tossed to and fro. At times like those there is little hope, and we are clinging to a floating raft with uncertainty as to how we will possibly make it through. Alas, there is hope, and it is found in Jesus Christ.

The sound of the ocean waves, the smell of salt water in the air, and the distinct breeze that can only come from the ocean always bring an instant calmness. As a child, the ocean became special to me during frequent trips with my parents to the coast. Those childhood trips to the beach gave way to a true love of the ocean as an adult. The shoreline became a peaceful refuge where my stress seemed to simply disappear. The older I get, the more I realize the peace I have found at the beach is actually wherever I go when I call on the name of Jesus Christ. Physically, being at the beach is where I still stand in awe at the stunning beauty God created in an ocean with waves that simply know how and where to stop. I am reminded of the scripture in Genesis that says,

"And God said, Let the waters under the heaven be gathered together unto one place, and let the dry land appear: and it was so. And God called the dry land Earth; and the

gathering together of the waters called he Seas: and God saw that it was good."

(GENESIS 1:9–10 KJV)

My trips to the beach are still frequent, but now they are with my wonderful husband who also follows Christ and finds refuge along the shore. We are blessed to watch our children form their own awe-inspired love for the beach and, at the same time, develop their own relationships with Christ. As I breathe the ocean air in and reflect on God and His wondrous works, I cannot help but agree with Him that indeed, all is good.

This book is written to help you find God's grace, beauty, and majesty one day at a time, when the tide is low.

CONTENTS

Special Thanks	*v*
Foreword	*ix*
The Lighthouse	1
Eyes on the Prize	3
Line in the Sand	7
Do Not Panic	9
Hiding Place	11
Irritants	13
Choose the Right Color	15
Shine On	19
New Territory	21
Revive	23
Fresh Start	27
Stacked	29
Treasure	31
The Gift of Peace	33
To God's Ears	37
Staying the Same	41
Suddenly	45
Peculiar	47
Clinging	51
Flock to the Beach	53
Broken Vessel	55
Broken Pieces	57
Up Close	59
Just Stand	63
Before the Storm	67
Jellyfish Stings	71
Forgiveness	75
Surfing	77
The Pier	81
Sharing	85
About the Author	*87*

THE LIGHTHOUSE

For centuries, the foghorn and lighthouse beacons have signaled the way to shore. At times, the fog that hovers over the ocean can be so thick that the captain of a ship has nothing else to rely on other than the strobe of light the lighthouse provides. The deep and mellow groan from the foghorn gives an audible signal to tread with caution but to continue steering forward. The horn warns that navigational hazards lie ahead, including the presence of other vessels. A captain may have coordinates mapped out and a thorough knowledge of the waterway, but help in the form of a guiding light and an audible sound is still needed.

In our daily lives, we sometimes have a map, plans, goals, and the timing all lined up, but every now and then chaos, confusion, worry, and stress can seemingly form all around us. It can appear as fog, so thick at times that it overwhelms and seems to overtake us. When we feel closed in by negativity, hopelessness, and despair, we need a guiding light. That light is found in Jesus Christ.

If we look to Christ to be our guide, He will surely lead the way. Christ is near to us by the indwelling of the Holy Spirit. That still, small voice of the Holy Spirit prompts us, whispers to us, and leads us if we listen. Some call it a gut feeling, others say it is our conscience speaking. However, as Christians, we know the good Lord lives in our hearts and leads, guides, and directs us. Scripture says, "For I know the plans I have for you, declares the Lord, plans to prosper you and not to harm you, plans to give you hope and a future." (Jeremiah 29:11 NIV) When life gets off course, know that with God leading the way, there is safety ahead.

Scripture:

> "Then spake Jesus again unto them, saying, I am the light of the world: he that followeth me shall not walk in darkness, but shall have the light of life."
>
> (JOHN 8:12 KJV)

CHAPTER 2

Eyes on the Prize

Have you ever walked along the beach after a terrible storm? There is typically debris lying around everywhere, pieces of driftwood, tons of broken shells—some rounded and some with sharp edges, tangled seaweed, dead jellyfish, and usually sunken-in sand holes that cause footsteps to be unleveled. All of these together makes a relaxing stroll along the beach considerably less than relaxing. You must watch where you step and how you step, and yet continue to move forward to your destination. You know the path, and you know the destination. You may even see it in the distance. However, you can also see the debris you must get through before reaching your goal.

Our steps in life can, at times, appear the same. We must watch where we step and how we step if we are conscious about our walk with Christ. There are times when it seems like the challenges of life are stacked so high that they block out the destination altogether. One day we may feel as though we are making great strides, then the next day feel like we are way off course, heading in a completely different direction! As a Christian, how do we keep going? How do we, in spite of the debris in our way, keep our chins up, our unwavering goals set, and our determination intact? It is simple: we turn to the promises of God. Scripture teaches us, *"These things I have spoken unto you, that in me ye might have peace. In the world ye shall have tribulation: but be of good cheer; I have overcome the world."* (John 16:33 KJV) We should *expect* challenges and hard times! Essentially, this scripture tells us there will most certainly be debris along the way that we will need to step over, dodge, or crawl through.

Let us be certain we pay attention to the most important part of that same scripture. Jesus says two very reassuring things: *"In me ye might have peace"* and *"I have overcome the world."* In other words, regardless of the debris, we can most certainly have peace and assurance that we can make it with victory on our side. Do you see your destination? Keep your eyes on it rather than on the debris. There is unspeakable joy waiting at the finish line.

Scripture:

> "Therefore, since we are surrounded by such a great cloud of witnesses, let us throw off everything that hinders and the sin that so easily entangles. And let us run with perseverance the race marked out for us, fixing our eyes on Jesus, the pioneer and perfecter of faith. For the joy set before him he endured the cross, scorning its shame, and sat down at the right hand of the throne of God. Consider him who endured such opposition from sinners, so that you will not grow weary and lose heart."
>
> (HEBREWS 12:1–3 NIV)

CHAPTER 3

LINE IN THE SAND

How does the ocean know exactly where to stop? Have you ever taken the time to really, *really* think about that? Each day across the entire planet, the ocean waves flow to the shore and then immediately recede. It is a constant, repetitive, and predictable action. Regardless of the continent, hemisphere, ocean or shore, the same thing happens day in and day out. The hand of God draws an invisible line in the sand that shows the waters how far to go. Just the mere thought of that is simply breathtaking and awe-inspiring.

In our daily lives, if we could just reflect on the image of that same invisible hand holding *our* hand, we would walk into each day, each situation, and each challenge with a totally different, yet positive perspective. We cannot see God visibly standing in front of us, but since we live by faith and not by sight, our faith in Him allows us to see Him in everything around us but only if we choose to look. Jeremiah 17:7–8 says, *"But blessed is the one who trusts in the Lord, whose confidence is in him. They will be like a tree planted by the water that sends out its roots by the stream. It does not fear when heat comes; its leaves are always green. It has no worries in a year of drought and never fails to bear fruit"* (NIV). The same great God who controls the shoreline is the same great God who holds us dear to His heart in the calm *and* rough seas of life.

Scripture:

> "The sea is His, for it was He who made it, And His hands formed the dry land. Come, let us worship and bow down, Let us kneel before the Lord our Maker."
>
> (PSALM 95:5–6 NIV)

CHAPTER 4

Do Not Panic

It is quite common in many movies to have a scene that shows a tiny boat springing a leak. There is typically one or two people in the boat who always seem to notice the leak at the worst possible time. In most of the scenes, the actors usually can pull out a bucket of some sort to scoop the water out of the bottom and pour it overboard. However, there are other times when they must resort to using their hands, scooping water out one handful at a time. Either way panic sets in, and the characters look to find hope in any direction that it could possibly be found.

Looking from the outside in, it is easy to ask a few seemingly obvious questions. Why didn't they check the overall condition of the boat, including a survey for holes, before they set sail? Why didn't they have some type of boat repair kit already onboard? Why would the sailors wait until they are in the middle of the ocean, in the midst of their problems, to try and come up with a solution?

Does that sound like your life? Do you wait until you are in the midst of a problem to then try and scramble around for a quick fix? There is an alternative solution that takes place before the problem arises. Put your hope and trust in the Lord upfront. Do not wait until you are in the middle of the ocean to scramble for a solution to your problem. *"Those who trust in themselves are fools, but those who walk in wisdom are kept safe."* (Proverbs 28:26 NIV) Lean on the Lord in the good days and every day. Then when the bad days come, you already have a loving relationship established and can fully rely on the Lord to lead you.

Scripture:

> "The LORD also will be a refuge for the oppressed, a refuge in times of trouble. And they that know thy name will put their trust in thee: for thou, LORD, hast not forsaken them that seek thee."
>
> (Psalm 9:9–10 KJV)

CHAPTER 5

HIDING PLACE

Oftentimes, as you walk along the water's edge, you can catch a quick glimpse of a tiny crab suddenly reverting back into its shell or into a hole in the sand. Whether it is from fear or simply as protection from the elements, the crab sees its shell or the hole as protection and as a hiding place. If you watch long enough, the crab uses a great level of patience and remains inside until it feels that all is safe in the outside world. Then it slowly emerges to pick up where it left off.

There are many times in life when we feel we need a place to hide from the world and its daily stresses. That feeling of hiding under the blanket, not wanting to face the day, can happen when we are overwhelmed or unsure how to handle the problems we are facing. Although we do not have a shell to hide us, we do have a Savior who has promised to be our refuge in the times of storms. He is only a prayer away and His word is accessible in the Bible, whether in the traditional book form or digital.

When you feel like you just cannot face what lies ahead of you, remember that you do indeed have a hiding place. Pray for the Lord's covering, peace, strength, and patience as you wait on the Lord to work all your troubles out for you. As Psalm 91:1–8 (NIV) says, *"Whoever dwells in the shelter of the Most High will rest in the shadow of the Almighty. I will say of the Lord, "He is my refuge and my fortress, my God, in whom I trust." Surely he will save you from the fowler's snare and from the deadly pestilence. He will cover you with his feathers, and under his wings you will find refuge; his faithfulness will be your shield and rampart. You will not fear the terror of night, nor the arrow that flies by day, nor the pestilence that stalks in the darkness, nor the plague that destroys at midday. A thousand may fall at your side, ten thousand at your right hand, but it will not come near you. You will only observe with your eyes and see the punishment of the wicked."*

Scripture:

> "You are my hiding place and my shield: I hope in your word."
>
> (PSALM 119:114 AKJV)

CHAPTER 6

IRRITANTS

It is quite fascinating to see oyster shells in a bay. They usually appear as grimy shells within a cluster of murk, mud, and debris from the sea. The oyster shells we see along the water's edge are intriguing *only* because we know the possibilities they hold inside. There has always been plenty of awe and mystery surrounding the formation of pearls. They can be thought of as seemingly "nothing" taking the shape of something quite special in the long run. Believe it or not, there is an extremely long process inside an oyster shell in order for a pearl to form and become the definition of stunning as we know it. The beauty of each pearl that was formed came from what was initially an irritant. It is simply amazing that something uncomfortable for the mollusk inside the oyster's shell actually transforms into an exquisite and precious stone.

How often in our daily lives do "irritants" seem to appear? How often does it seem we have a plan in place that seemingly goes off track? Sometimes we can see so clearly how life would be better if… if things were different—if the job paid more, if the sickness left, or if the relationship was better. There are a lot of "ifs" to fill in that gap for everyone at some point in life. Have you ever stopped to think that those so-called irritants are working out for your good? Romans 8:28 says, *"And we know that in all things God works for the good of those who love him, who have been called according to his purpose."* That initial irritant in the oyster's shell was absolutely the only way a pearl could form. In your life, the good and the bad together are absolutely the only way to form the person that God already knows you will become.

Scripture:

> "He has made everything beautiful in its time. He has also set eternity in the human heart; yet no one can fathom what God has done from beginning to end."
>
> (ECCLESIASTES 3:11 NIV)

CHAPTER 7

CHOOSE THE RIGHT COLOR

Have you ever paid attention to the fact that depending upon where you are on the coastline, the color of the ocean appears visibly different? For example, you can walk along the eastern USA shore, around the North Carolina coast, and see grayish-colored ocean water that appears to be a bit murky. You can head due south and continue to walk along the same east coast, but in Florida . . . the ocean water will appear to be more vibrant and green. Same body of water, same coastline, theoretically the same ocean water but a totally different color. How can that be?

It actually takes more than a shared continental coastline to interpret what impacts the colors of the ocean. Just as the terrain changes from neighborhood to neighborhood and from state to state, so does the terrain of the ocean's floor. The depth of the ocean at any given point, the reflection of sunlight, the salinity, and the microorganisms found in the ocean can all play a huge role in how the ocean colors appear to the human eye. Therefore, in essence, the color of the ocean is determined by what is actually happening "in" the ocean at that point in time.

Today, what is *happening* in your life that seems to be a challenge? In every challenging situation, there are always outcomes and consequences to our choices and reactions to those challenges. The choices we make in the midst of those hard situations are mostly played out in front of others . . . family, friends, coworkers, or neighbors, etc. At some point, we all need someone to turn to for advice, help, or for simply a listening ear. Admitting we need help can be hard and can easily give way to feelings of vulnerability. It is crucial that we seek out the best person on whom to lean. Just like the happenings *in* the ocean determine its color . . . who a person is on the inside and what they have experienced in life determines what is reflected on the outside.

Adequately choosing who to turn to can be tough and requires discernment and evidences of a person who can really step in and help. Matthew 7:16–18 says, "*By their fruit you will recognize them. Are grapes gathered from thorn bushes, or figs from thistles? Likewise, every good tree bears good fruit, but a bad tree bears bad fruit. A good tree cannot bear bad fruit, and a bad tree cannot bear good fruit.*" When you are trying to determine who to turn to in the midst of a challenging time or crisis—be sure to turn to those who are most equipped to help you, gently guide and lovingly lead you in the right direction. Evaluate his or her life story and look for indications of a person who has good fruit and the love of Christ on the inside. Who a person is on the inside will determine his or her outward actions and will also determine who you actually see in front of you.

Scripture:

"As water reflects the face, so one's life reflects the heart."
(Proverbs 27:19 NIV)

CHAPTER 8

SHINE ON

The morning light that shines as the sun rises across the ocean is simply stunning. It sends a glow across the water that glistens, sparkles, and dances with the movement of the ocean's waves. The sun provides the light as we see it become visibly brighter and higher into the morning sky. The sun sends light across a portion of the ocean at first, seemingly creating a path of reflection. The longer we keep our eyes on the morning sun, the higher it goes and the larger it becomes. As it rises higher and higher, it also begins to spread a brightness not only across the ocean but the entire sky.

Sometimes there are challenges in life that tend to take all of our focus, time, and attention. If we spend too much time focused on what is wrong, we can easily slip into feeling the doom and gloom of hopelessness, sadness, and defeat. Then, my God, if we just keep our eyes on You, Your mercy, grace, peace and comfort shine on us. You will keep us on the right path and in perfect peace. The more we follow You, the more we understand that we cannot make it without You. The more we focus on You, the more we understand that You and You alone can light our paths. You can give us hope and you can shine your love in our hearts.

Scripture:

> "The LORD is my light and my salvation; whom shall I fear? The LORD is the strength of my life; of whom shall I be afraid?"

CHAPTER 9

New Territory

No matter how many times I go to the beach, seeing footprints from someone walking along earlier leaves an impression, literally. Those footprints in the sand indicate a "newness" of sorts and mean that all of the old impressions have been washed away. It means the waves have wiped the slate clean. Being the first to leave footprints all over again feels like I am setting the course and treading new territory.

In life, treading new territory can be daunting. Each footprint may be filled with triumphs and failures, mountaintops and valleys, tears or smiles. Starting out on new adventures can oftentimes give way to hesitation. New jobs, relocating, marriage, divorce, births, deaths, and unexpected changes in life can simply take an overwhelming turn. We must take refuge in knowing that God loves us, sees us, and knows our situations—even before they become situations. With one foot in front of the other, we can get through life. Simply live life one moment at a time … one day at a time, and as scripture says in Philippians 4:6, while being anxious for nothing—in old or new territory.

Scripture:

> "The Lord himself goes before you and will be with you; he will never leave you nor forsake you. Do not be afraid; do not be discouraged."
>
> (Deuteronomy 31:8 NIV)

CHAPTER 10

REVIVE

Seeing pieces of driftwood and debris wash up on shore is common. The wood usually appears old, crinkled, worn, and unusable. It is now seemingly discarded and simply enduring the crashing waves and elements of nature. Yet, if you really stop to think about it, each piece of driftwood, at some time or another, had a story. It was a part of something much larger and served a totally different or greater purpose. Driftwood along the shore may have been part of an old wooden vessel, a building or structure of some sort, lost cargo, branches, or even an entire tree! Regardless, it has now landed in a different season of life and needs only a new perspective. Believe it or not, even in its seemingly useless condition, the driftwood can be dried out, revived, and utilized for all new purposes.

As the years move along, each of our bodies and minds will begin to age and continue to age. There are very visible signs that are hard to mistake as anything other than natural aging—gray hair, wrinkles, slower steps, and delayed thought processes are just a few. It is easy to slip into a sad and reflective state of mind about what we accomplished during our younger years. Those heydays of yesteryears can seem like such distant memories that are quickly fading. We must remember, however, that the same God who kept us during our youth is the same God who will keep us as we age. With a firm foundation in Christ and a perspective given directly from scripture, we can be revived and utilized for even greater things as we get older. Philippians 1:6 says, *"For I am confident of this, that He who began a good work in you will continue to perfect it until the day of Christ Jesus."* You felt important and needed in your youth, and guess what? God can continue to use and perfect you as you age.

In actuality, our age, mental, and physical capabilities have nothing to do with God's ability to use us for His glory. We just need to stand firm as a willing vessel in every season of our life. *"The righteous man will flourish like the palm tree, He will grow like a cedar in Lebanon. Planted in the house of the LORD, They will flourish in the courts of our God. They will still yield fruit in old age; They shall be full of sap and very green."* (Psalm 92:12–14). There is much beauty, wisdom, and purpose still to be found in those who are aging.

Scripture:

> Even to your old age and gray hairs I am he, I am he who will sustain you. I have made you and I will carry you; I will sustain you and I will rescue you.
>
> (ISAIAH 46:4)

CHAPTER 11

FRESH START

The sea stars or "starfishes" as they are most commonly called, are intriguing creatures. They are unique in every aspect of their lives. There are around 2,000 different species of sea stars, and they are visibly identifiable by, typically, their five points. However, some variations of sea stars can have up to forty points! Another interesting fact about sea stars is that instead of blood running through their circulatory systems, they have filtered water. Water from the ocean runs through their bodies, not blood. These are pretty amazing facts about sea stars that may be little known to some. Yet, one sea star fact stands above the rest: they have the ability to regenerate their limbs. Even more surprising is that a few of the sea star species can actually regenerate the entire body from only one limb. The regeneration process is not quick and can take anywhere from months to a year or more. What a fascinating concept to ponder.

As Christian believers, we do not have the ability to regenerate our bodies the exact same way a sea star does. However, through Christ, we have been given a generous gift of forgiveness and grace. Each of those gifts is priceless and allows us to begin each day anew. Our facial features and body will look the same, but our hearts and spirit can be renewed. Made a mistake? Made a bad choice? Feel like you need a fresh start? Bring your honest heart to the Lord. *"You were taught, with regard to your former way of life, to put off your old self, which is being corrupted by its deceitful desires; to be made new in the attitude of your minds; and to put on the new self, created to be like God in true righteousness and holiness."* (Ephesians 4:22–24) You can ask the Lord to create in you a clean heart and renew your mind in the ways of the Lord. He can truly give you a new start indeed.

Scripture:

> "But this I call to mind, and therefore I have hope: The steadfast love of the Lord never ceases; his mercies never come to an end; they are new every morning; great is your faithfulness."
>
> (LAMENTATIONS 3: 21–23 ESV)

CHAPTER 12

STACKED

When the sandbags are filled and stacked along the ocean's shoreline, it typically means the conditions for flooding are favorable and erosion can occur. The concept of sandbags is nothing more than a preventative measure that has been in place for centuries. At the ocean, or within low areas prone to floods, the sandbags simply prevent or limit flooding. Commonly used burlap or polypropylene bags are partially filled with sand and then stacked atop each other to form a barrier. Interestingly enough, the actual sand in the bag itself is not what keeps the flood at bay. The porous fabric of the bags allow each bag to capture all types of particles mixed in the floodwaters like silt and clay and, together with the sand, forms a heavy barrier. The heavier the bag of sand gets with the added particles, the less water can actually flow into the bag, the more protection in place from flooding damage.

In life, we need to be proactive to handle the damage that can come into our lives and purposefully not adopt a worldview. Going through life unintentionally living like everyone else can lead you down the wrong path. Scripture says, *"Enter through the narrow gate. For wide is the gate and broad is the road that leads to destruction, and many enter through it."* (Matthew 7:13 NIV) Just as sandbags are used as preventative measures, we can turn to the book of Proverbs to gain practical insight and wisdom for all that we encounter daily. The book of Proverbs is easily applicable for making decisions about our attitudes, relationships, finances, etc. Each verse should be "stacked up" and referenced so that we know how to handle life before the floods come. If we study God's word daily, we not only build a closer relationship with Him but we also gain the wisdom He so freely gives if we seek it. We should allow Him to fill our heats with His love, and we should stack up all of the scriptures in our heart!

Scripture:

"Wisdom is a shelter as money is a shelter, but the advantage of knowledge is this: Wisdom preserves those who have it."

(ECCLESIASTES 7:12 NIV)

CHAPTER 13

TREASURE

When shipwrecked, the vast treasures and shimmering gold onboard sink and remain submerged, but they do not disappear. The gold retains value even when hidden in mud and mixed up in the debris from the wreck. Whenever found, whether a day later or many years into the future, the gold's value is still there. Furthermore, in some cases over time the value actually increases.

In life, we can become shipwrecked and stray off course from our calling and intended path. How do we get back on track? That is the million-dollar question. Nobody wants to be off track. Nobody wants to feel unproductive or insignificant, and nobody wants to walk around aimlessly not fulfilling the very thing they were created to do and be!

What is the solution? Let's get to the heart of the matter. A relationship with Christ is the only resolution that will sustain a person during any shipwrecked season of life. Going through this type of season requires patience, focus, and an unmovable faith to keep us grounded. Scripture says, *"Holding on to faith and a good conscience, which some have rejected and so have suffered shipwreck with regard to the faith."* (1 Timothy 1:19 NIV)

Constant prayer and meditation on God's word with a fervent heart that desires to walk with Christ is what turns a shipwreck into found treasure. In our lives, getting off track does not have to mean staying off track! God can purposefully turn our debris of bad choices, clutter of mistakes, muddy, unclear minds, shameful sins, and broken fragments of despair into something completely worthy of immense value. That newfound value, rooted in grace, can then fulfill us and yet be far-reaching into the lives of others, making what we have to offer and share even more valuable than before.

Scripture:

> "In all this you greatly rejoice, though now for a little while you may have had to suffer grief in all kinds of trials. These have come so that the proven genuineness of your faith—of greater worth than gold, which perishes even though refined by fire—may result in praise, glory and honor when Jesus Christ is revealed."
>
> (1 PETER 1:6–7 NIV)

CHAPTER 14

THE GIFT OF PEACE

How do we recognize when there is a peaceful breeze over the ocean? Is it by the calming sound of the waves as they make intermittent laps and splashes along the beach? Is it simply the sight of an ocean with waters that seem to gently sway at a distance, or is it the feel of a gentle breeze as you stand by the ocean's edge to breathe it all in? Regardless of how you define peace at the ocean, it is quite recognizable and distinct by its sound, by its sight, and by its touch. That peace can be recognizable anywhere.

In my early twenties, well before I became a mother, I had a very distinct experience that I consider a huge gift of peace. As a young woman, sadly I was close friends with worry and anxiety. I would worry about how the bills would be paid, how relationships would go, how each day at work would progress, and how life in general would go from one day to the next. One particular evening I remember worrying about a small medical procedure I needed to have the following day. I was so worried that I tossed and turned in my bed and just simply could not sleep. I knew even all those years ago that God was very much a part of my life and that I could indeed turn it all over to him. I just needed to be able to hand my worry and troubles over to the Lord *completely*. That night, I knew my worry had reached a high level of concern, so, alone in my dark room, I cried out to the Lord to take my worry away. All of a sudden, I could feel peace around me so thick that I sat up in my bed immediately. I felt as though there was something most certainly there for me to see. The peace of the Lord was literally all around me in such a way that I could feel it. It was just as though I had been placed in the middle of the most comfortable blanket of cotton you could ever imagine. I could even "hear" the peace—there was such a calm surrounding me that it seemed to affect every sense I had. I stared for a while in complete amazement because it was such a moment of awe. And I was truly thankful.

I think back to that experience from time to time and I am instantly back in the middle of that blanket of "cotton", still oh so very grateful. I feel as though I was given a personal glimpse of what God's peace is like in a time when I needed it most. I remember that night and I use those memories as a great reminder of just how close God is and how he can and does answer prayers. Scripture says, "*And the peace of God, which transcends all understanding, will guard your hearts and your minds in Christ Jesus.*" (Philippians 4:7 NIV) I could not understand *how* His peace surrounded me, but I knew it was in such a way that all of my worry immediately left. I am 100 percent convinced that the Lord answered my prayer for peace in a way that did absolutely transcend my understanding. Years later I still can't adequately explain what happened, but I can say it was truly beautiful, serene, and a true gift of peace from a loving God.

God can quiet any storm with but one word. Remember that as you stand looking at the rough waters that appear from time to time in life.

Scripture:

> "He got up, rebuked the wind and said to the waves, 'Quiet! Be still!' Then the wind died down and it was completely calm."
>
> (Mark 4:39 NIV)

CHAPTER 15

To God's Ears

How many times have we stood by the water's edge and simply tossed pebbles into the water? Pebble after pebble after pebble we toss them in as far as our arm's length and strength will allow. Once the pebbles hit the water's surface they sink beyond our physical sight, but we know without a shadow of a doubt the pebbles will hit the bottom. We never see how it happens but we know it lands. If we practice, we can increase our strength and technique in tossing each pebble further and further. It does not matter if we toss the pebble near or far; as long as we do not give up in reaching the water, the pebble will make it in. Whether we have weak arm strength or the arm strength of a professional baseball pitcher, we know once our pebble hits the water, it truly is on its way to the ocean's floor.

The faith we use in prayer works the same way. We pray daily recognizing who our sovereign God is, and we pray with a heart of thanksgiving. In addition, there are prayers for help, prayers for loved ones, prayers for big things, and even prayers for little things. As Christians, it is our joyful duty to always pray with a thankful heart as we live life aligned to scripture. We are to always pray genuinely from our hearts. We do not physically see our prayers enter God's ears, but if our faith is truly in the Lord, we know they do. Scripture says, *"The Lord is near to all who call on him, to all who call on him in truth."* (Psalm 145:18 NIV) To strengthen our prayers, we can use the model prayer Jesus provided for His Disciples: *"And it came to pass, that, as he was praying in a certain place, when he ceased, one of his disciples said unto him, Lord, teach us to pray, as John also taught his disciples. "And he said unto them, When ye pray, say, Our Father which art in heaven, Hallowed be thy name. Thy kingdom come. Thy will be done, as in heaven, so in earth. Give us day by day our daily bread. And forgive us our sins; for we also forgive every one that is indebted to us. And lead us not into temptation; but deliver us from evil."* (Luke 11:1–4 KJV)

Whether a person is new to the Christian faith with little experience in praying or a seasoned believer with many, many years of praying, a prayer prayed in truth and in the belief of Christ does reach the Lord.

Scripture:

> "Then Jesus told his disciples a parable to show them that they should always pray and not give up."
>
> (Luke 18:1 NIV)

CHAPTER 16

STAYING THE SAME

Projections about the progression of shoreline erosion are not showing favorable for coastlines to remain visibly the same in years to come. The constant lapping of waves storm after storm and day after day eventually break down the sediment structure along each shoreline to slowly change the appearance of where the ocean starts and where the beach ends. There will always be the separation of the ocean from the sand; however, through all endured, the shoreline simply continues to look different with each passing year.

In our lives as Christians, we should strive for something similar…. We need to stand firm in life and remain the same storm after storm and day after day. Although we may begin to look differently as we age and as we weather life's many trials and tribulations, we should remain the same in our hearts. Challenges over time can come with losing loved ones, facing or witnessing in others the daily struggles life brings, simple and large-scale disappointments, and even daily negativity from newscasters on every broadcast. With each intake of worldly information, each personal witness of hardship, each seemingly step backward, we must be careful to stay in communion with the Lord. Our prayer must be to God, simply asking Him daily to *"create in me a pure heart, O God, and renew a steadfast spirit within me. Do not cast me from your presence or take your Holy Spirit from me. Restore to me the joy of your salvation and grant me a willing spirit, to sustain me."* (Psalm 51:10–12 NIV)

With each victory that the Lord carries us through, we should gain an even more grateful heart that seeks after God, and we should gain a stronger faith and hope. *"Therefore, since we have been justified through faith, we have peace with God through our Lord Jesus Christ, through whom we have gained access by faith into this grace in which we now stand. And we boast in the hope of the glory of God. Not only so, but we also glory in our sufferings, because we know that suffering produces perseverance; perseverance, character; and character, hope. And hope does not put us to shame, because God's love has been poured out into our hearts through the Holy Spirit, who has been given to us."* (Romans 5:1–5 KJV)

Things may appear to be in a constant state of change with seemingly uncertainty and visible differences all around us. However, it is essential to remember that God has everything under control. This includes our day-to-day lives, the lives of those around us, the land and sea, and all that is in, around, above, and below the Earth.

Scripture:

> "Should you not fear me?" declares the LORD. "Should you not tremble in my presence? I made the sand a boundary for the sea, an everlasting barrier it cannot cross. The waves may roll, but they cannot prevail; they may roar, but they cannot cross it."
>
> (JEREMIAH 5:22 NIV)

CHAPTER 17

SUDDENLY

Picture this: it is a beautiful, sunlit day at your favorite beach. You decide to park the car and take a stroll that turns into a 3-mile walk along the shoreline. The walk is quiet, peaceful, and uneventful, and the more you walk, the more your mind seems to relax. The breeze blowing across your face is warm with a slight mist from the waves you pass along the way. As you continue your stroll, you dangle your shoes from your hands and feel the warm sand between your toes with each step. The seagulls are hovering above like always, and there seem to be a lot of beachgoers napping underneath their colorful umbrellas. The sun's beam is bright and provides a beautiful path of light across the middle of your ocean view. You feel as though all is right with the world, and the more you walk, the more confident you become in your abilities to work out any problem that should ever come your way.

Then, without warning, the seagulls all fly off into the distance, the sun quickly moves behind a cloud, the sky seems to instantly darken, and the slight breeze you felt earlier changes to increasing gusts of wind. Where did this sudden storm come from? How will you make it back to your car, which at this point seems millions of miles away?

Most everyone in life has been faced with a scenario, such as the following: life is going great; everything has fallen into place in all areas and then, without warning, a storm filled with crisis shows up. The solution seems a million miles away. How in the world do you get through something you were not expecting?

It is simple: you rely on the strength of the Lord. His strength gives you courage, peace, a steadfastness to remain strong, and wisdom to think clearly. No need to fear or tremble. *"Do not be anxious about anything, but in every situation, by prayer and petition, with thanksgiving, present your requests to God."* (Philippians 4:6 NIV) Through prayer, thanksgiving, and trust, follow how the Lord leads you through every storm.

Scripture:

> "I keep my eyes always on the Lord. With him at my right hand, I will not be shaken."
>
> (PSALM 16:8 NIV)

CHAPTER 18

PECULIAR

There is a vast number of fish in the ocean—big fish, little fish, colorful fish, and even transparent fish. There are common types of fish that everyone knows the names, like salmon, trout, flounder, tilapia, snapper, catfish, etc. There are also types of fish in the ocean that are lesser known and definitely intriguing due to their character traits. Puffer fish fall into this category, as do seahorses. Let us not forget the beautifully accented trigger fish (that can crush shells with its mouth) or the extraordinarily beautifully-colored Mandarinfish. What about the lanternfish? It has the ability to produce its own light! These intriguing fish are still fish, but they obviously stand out from the crowd.

What about us as Christians? We are human like everyone else, but we are supposed to stand out from the crowd as well. Scripture says, *"But ye are a chosen generation, a royal priesthood, an holy nation, a peculiar people; that ye should shew forth the praises of him who hath called you out of darkness into his marvelous light: Which in time past were not a people, but are now the people of God: which had not obtained mercy, but now have obtained mercy."* (1 Peter 2:9–10)

Unlike those who do not follow Christ, we should exhibit daily the fruit of the spirit. *"But the fruit of the Spirit is love, joy, peace, forbearance, kindness, goodness, faithfulness, gentleness and self-control. Against such things there is no law. Those who belong to Christ Jesus have crucified the flesh with its passions and desires. Since we live by the Spirit, let us keep in step with the Spirit. Let us not become conceited, provoking and envying each other."* (Galatians 5:22–25 NIV)

Just like those fish that seem to be out of the ordinary they are still classified as fish, but their characteristics make them stand out significantly. As Christians, we too need to stand out because of our character traits that imitate Christ.

Scripture:

> "For the grace of God that bringeth salvation hath appeared to all men, Teaching us that, denying ungodliness and worldly lusts, we should live soberly, righteously, and godly, in this present world; Looking for that blessed hope, and the glorious appearing of the great God and our Saviour Jesus Christ; Who gave himself for us, that he might redeem us from all iniquity, and purify unto himself a peculiar people, zealous of good works."
>
> (TITUS 2:11–14 KJV)

CHAPTER 19

Clinging

The last thing passengers on any boat want to do is find themselves clinging to an inflatable swim ring for dear life. Yet it happens—in TV shows, in movies, and in real life. In an instant, a peaceful or otherwise controlled boat ride can turn into a moment of frenzy and uncertainty, a moment where holding on has never been more important.

In life, when the challenges we face are seemingly at an all-time high, we need to cling to our hope and faith in the Lord with a sincere belief that His promises will always remain true. It is in those times of hardship, sadness, grief, uncertainty, and even loneliness that we must cling with all our heart, with all our soul, with all our strength, and with all our mind. We must cling to God's unchanging hands ... the hands and arms that will hold us because we cannot hold ourselves. We must cling to the One who gives us rest, mercy, love, forgiveness, and grace.

We must hold on to Jesus like our life depends on it ... because it does.

Scripture:

> "He gives strength to the weary
> and increases the power of the weak.
> Even youths grow tired and weary,
> and young men stumble and fall;
> But those who hope in the Lord
> will renew their strength.
> They will soar on wings like eagles;
> they will run and not grow weary,
> they will walk and not be faint."
>
> (ISAIAH 40:29–31 NIV)

CHAPTER 20

FLOCK TO THE BEACH

How is it possible that millions of people flock to beaches every single year to simply lie in the sand, stare at the ocean, and relax? What is it about the ocean that causes many to take a break from the normal hustle and bustle of life? What is it about gazing at the line where the oceans and sky meet that seems to quiet our minds? What is it about the beaming sun, the warm sand, and the methodical sound of the ocean's waves that cause us to sit in silence? Why do we pack up our families, sometimes multiple times a year, to simply watch nature at its finest? For those who truly love the beach, the answer is complicated yet simple.

There is an awe and a natural connection to what God has so lovingly created. Nature surrounds us, and nature is an obvious and visible statement to what God has created for us to enjoy and appreciate. The division point of nature between the ocean and land is an amazing testament to God's handiwork. Scripture teaches us, "*And God said, Let the waters under the heaven be gathered together unto one place, and let the dry land appear: and it was so. And God called the dry land Earth; and the gathering together of the waters called he Seas: and God saw that it was good.*" (Genesis 1:9–10 NIV)

As we sit upon the shore to relax and enjoy the creativity of God's hands, let us find the beautiful scenery of nature, yet another reason to praise the Lord. God Himself saw that it was a good thing to behold! Therefore, he passed along that same appreciation to those of us who love the beach as well.

Scripture:

> "In his hand are the depths of the earth,
> and the mountain peaks belong to him.
> The sea is his, for he made it,
> and his hands formed the dry land."
>
> (PSALM 95:4–5 NIV)

CHAPTER 21

BROKEN VESSEL

How would it make you feel to watch your favorite boat being torn away from the dock during a storm, paint and siding literally peeling off, metal bending, interior torn, leaving the boat completely dismantled shred by shred? What happens if it gets even worse? If it was not already bad enough, you watch in disbelief as thieves come by and salvage any parts they think will bring value if sold! What do you do when you watch the destruction happen right in front of your eyes?

You stand firm in the knowledge that this is just a moment in time and that things will indeed get better. You may not have a clue *how* things will get better, but you hold onto your faith and you recall the words of scripture you have written on your heart.

If the boat scenario parallels something happening in your life right now, you should most certainly look at the situation not with your natural eyes but through spiritual eyes. *"Though an host should encamp against me, my heart shall not fear: though war should rise against me, in this will I be confident."* (Psalm 27:3 KJV)

Scripture:

> "I remain confident of this: I will see the goodness of the Lord in the land of the living. Wait for the Lord; be strong and take heart and wait for the Lord."
>
> (PSALM 27:13–14 NIV)

CHAPTER 22

BROKEN PIECES

By the time those amazingly beautiful seashells reach the point where we can bend down and pick them up out of the sand, they are oftentimes jagged, broken, and crushed into pieces. Many people consider it a gem when an entire seashell is found along the shore. The intricate details of those seashells found in pieces are just as beautiful. They are still unique, they still have a story, they are still identifiable, and they are still God's creation.

In life hard times come and, as a result, we feel broken. Our heart can feel as though it has been crushed into pieces. If we lean on the Lord, we can make it through. He will pour out His love, His strength, His peace, and His stamina. During those hard times in life, we develop a testimony of God's grace. Our stories are being written. We are still identifiable but we become refined. We may be worn, but we are still His wonderfully made creation. The beauty of those experiences of God's grace and mercy that come from tribulation can be found when we share our testimony and help those who face similar circumstances and challenges.

Scripture:

> "The Lord is close to the brokenhearted and saves those who are crushed in spirit."
>
> (PSALM 34:18 NIV)

CHAPTER 23

UP CLOSE

Have you ever looked at sand under a microscope? It is pretty amazing and simply beautiful. Each individual grain of sand has its own shape, texture, and color. Yet, when walking along the beach as far as the eye can see, sand looks like it is all the same.

How does sand even become sand? Sand is the result of varying oceanic materials mingled together, including shells, rocks, minerals such as quartz, feldspar, and mica, and marine life skeletons. Over time, the effects of weather, waves, currents, and erosion cause these particles to be broken down by microorganisms in the ocean.

When you stop to examine a handful of sand microscopically, you quickly find that every grain is actually unique with its own story of how it ended up as sand.

Our lives here on Earth are similar. Viewed in a stadium full of people, we as humans appear to be all the same … just people. As a group, there are many things we all do alike. However, if you begin to study each person in the crowd individually, you will quickly find there is an intricate story lying beneath the surface. As God's children, we are quite unique and truly stand out from the crowd. We are all purposefully made and known by the Lord. The book of Psalms says, *"For you created my inmost being; you knit me together in my mother's womb. I praise you because I am fearfully and wonderfully made; your works are wonderful, I know that full well. My frame was not hidden from you when I was made in the secret place, when I was woven together in the depths of the earth. Your eyes saw my unformed body; all the days ordained for me were written in your book before one of them came to be."* (139:13–16 NIV)

Simply stated, God knows everything about us, and He knew it before we were even formed in our mother's womb. He cares about us, and He cares about the big things in our lives as well as the little things. *"And even the very hairs of your head are all numbered."* (Matthew 10:30 NIV)

Never doubt the love of our Heavenly Father. Just as the grains of sand are unique and beyond measure, so are God's thoughts towards each of us.

Scripture:

> "How precious to me are your thoughts, God! How vast is the sum of them! Were I to count them, they would outnumber the grains of sand - when I awake, I am still with you."
>
> (PSALM 139:17–18 NIV)

CHAPTER 24

Just Stand

It is quite amazing to feel the rush of ripples and small waves around your ankles. On a warm, sunny day, the coolness of the ocean water feels simply refreshing. However, if you stand there for very long, it becomes more than an amazing feeling: it becomes effort. With the onset of each rushing wave, the sand beneath your feet begins to wash away, making your stance unleveled. It quickly turns into a determined grip to keep your balance as more and more waves approach. With your leg muscles braced and your arms steadied at each side, you wait for the next wave... and the next. Then, suddenly, you notice that enough waves have washed around your feet that they have become planted in the wet sand and, once again, you have become grounded.

Think about hardships in life. They spring up suddenly, seemingly from nowhere. Bright sunny days can quickly turn into what feels like warfare with the challenges that arise. Wave after wave of trials and tribulations seem to rush around you, and with each new layer and level of hardship you must hold onto your faith as a Christian, tighter and tighter. As the saying goes, you must dig your heels in and absolutely refuse to give up hope... the one true Hope, our Lord and Savior Jesus Christ.

"Therefore being justified by faith, we have peace with God through our Lord Jesus Christ: By whom also we have access by faith into this grace wherein we stand, and rejoice in hope of the glory of God. And not only so, but we glory in tribulations also: knowing that tribulation worketh patience; And patience, experience; and experience, hope: And hope maketh not ashamed; because the love of God is shed abroad in our hearts by the Holy Ghost which is given unto us."

(Romans 5:1–5 KJV)

No matter what comes your way, simply stand. *"Therefore, my brethren dearly beloved and longed for, my joy and crown, so stand fast in the Lord, my dearly beloved."* (Philippians 4:1 KJV)

The Lord's mercies are new every morning. God does fight our battles. We just need to seek strength in Him, stand firm in Him, and let His will be done. Simply anchor your soul in the Lord. Life will, once again, become leveled.

Scripture:

> "Finally, be strong in the Lord and in his mighty power. Put on the full armor of God, so that you can take your stand against the devil's schemes. For our struggle is not against flesh and blood, but against the rulers, against the authorities, against the powers of this dark world and against the spiritual forces of evil in the heavenly realms. Therefore put on the full armor of God, so that when the day of evil comes, you may be able to stand your ground, and after you have done everything, to stand. Stand firm then, with the belt of truth buckled around your waist, with the breastplate of righteousness in place, and with your feet fitted with the readiness that comes from the gospel of peace. In addition to all this, take up the shield of faith, with which you can extinguish all the flaming arrows of the evil one. Take the helmet of salvation and the sword of the Spirit, which is the word of God.
>
> And pray in the Spirit on all occasions with all kinds of prayers and requests. With this in mind, be alert and always keep on praying for all the Lord's people."
>
> (EPHESIANS 6:10:18 NIV)

CHAPTER 25

BEFORE THE STORM

E ver planned a weeklong beach "vacay" and the clear, sunny skies forecast unexpectedly changes on the same day that you arrive? The meteorologist gives surprising news that the warm breeze and blue skies you have today will soon change to a life-threatening storm that just developed over the ocean, and the storm is now rapidly on the way. Wow. Talk about change. How do you handle it? The storm has not arrived yet, but you *know* it's coming and there is only so much you can do. Where do you start with the preparation? What should you do first?

In life, the bad news does not always appear simply from one moment to the next. Sometimes the bad news is delivered long before the challenge itself actually arrives. Finding out that your employer will have mass layoffs over the next six months or seeing that the damage done to your home by a recent hurricane is so severe the home has to be completely rebuilt with no help from the insurance company or being diagnosed with a sickness or disease that has no cure ... all examples of bad news before the actual challenge arrives.

Scripture says, *"Be anxious for nothing, but in everything, by prayer and petition, with thanksgiving, present your requests to God. And the peace of God, which surpasses all understanding, will guard your hearts and your minds in Christ Jesus."* (Philippians 4:6–7 NIV) Essentially, this scripture teaches us that there is no need to worry. As a believer, everything can be taken to God in prayer with requests. All the while, maintain a heart of thanksgiving. Remain thankful that God is who He says He is. Remain thankful that God has given us the gift of prayer. Remain thankful that the prayers of the righteous are indeed heard by the Lord according to Proverbs 15:29.

Regardless of how close or how far away a storm of life is, lean on the Lord. Be confident in Him. Write the scriptures upon your heart. Know that the Lord God *"is able to do infinitely more than all we ask or imagine, according to His power that is at work within us, to Him be the glory in the church and in Christ Jesus throughout*

all generations, forever and ever. Amen." (Ephesians 3:20–21 NIV)
Do you see a storm on the horizon? Rest in the Lord.

Scripture:

> "Therefore I tell you, do not worry about your life, what
> you will eat or drink; or about your body, what you will
> wear. Is not life more than food, and the body more than
> clothes? Look at the birds of the air; they do not sow or
> reap or store away in barns, and yet your heavenly Father
> feeds them. Are you not much more valuable than they?
> Can any one of you by worrying add a single hour to
> your life?
>
> And why do you worry about clothes? See how the
> flowers of the field grow. They do not labor or spin. Yet
> I tell you that not even Solomon in all his splendor was
> dressed like one of these. If that is how God clothes the
> grass of the field, which is here today and tomorrow is
> thrown into the fire, will he not much more clothe you—
> you of little faith? So do not worry, saying, 'What shall we
> eat?' or 'What shall we drink?' or 'What shall we wear?'
> For the pagans run after all these things, and your heav-
> enly Father knows that you need them. But seek first his
> kingdom and his righteousness, and all these things will
> be given to you as well. Therefore do not worry about
> tomorrow, for tomorrow will worry about itself. Each
> day has enough trouble of its own."
>
> (MATTHEW 6:25–34 NIV)

CHAPTER 26

JELLYFISH STINGS

Much too often, beachgoers are frolicking in the ocean water with not a care in the world, and, suddenly, seemingly out of nowhere, a jellyfish appears with a vicious sting. What started off as a fun dip in the ocean can quickly turn into pain with venomous stingers left in the skin and a possible trip to the emergency room. The common solution is to rinse the affected area with saltwater and vinegar. Sounds pretty simple since saltwater is readily available at the beach, and adding vinegar to the first aid kit is quick and easy as long as you remember to plan ahead.

Isn't that just like life sometimes? All is going well, routines are in place, and seemingly everything is going just as it should. Then, without warning, a crisis, a trial, or a "sting" appears, bringing the sense of serenity to an abrupt halt. It seems to catch us by surprise, but should it? If we believe scripture to be true, then trials and tribulations become expected.

"Be joyful in hope, patient in affliction, faithful in prayer."
(ROMANS 12:12 NIV)

This scripture gives us specific advice in handling the hard times, challenges, trials, and "stings," which indeed come to our doorstep.

Those jellyfish stings can be a small and temporary problem, and the fun day at the beach can continue after proper attention and treatment, but day-after-day, week-after-week, and month-after-month, those small stinger problems can seem to add up if not treated correctly! Remembering the words of scripture, resting in God's promises to us, and keeping a joyful attitude during those hard times can make all the difference in how you get through problems that arise.

Scripture:

"Consider it pure joy, my brothers and sisters, whenever you face trials of many kinds, because you know that the testing of your faith produces perseverance. Let perseverance finish its work so that you may be mature and complete, not lacking anything. If any of you lacks wisdom, you should ask God, who gives generously to all without finding fault, and it will be given to you. But when you ask, you must believe and not doubt, because the one who doubts is like a wave of the sea, blown and tossed by the wind. That person should not expect to receive anything from the Lord. Such a person is double-minded and unstable in all they do."

(JAMES 1:2–8 NIV)

CHAPTER 27

FORGIVENESS

How many times have you seen a person lose something in a wave, a ring, a watch, a necklace, or even a wallet? One minute the item is in the person's possession but the next minute, the item has slipped away quickly into the ocean's fast-moving current. There is typically an onset of instant panic, frantic searching in nearby water, and then a realization that the item is gone, permanently. It can bring immediate reflection, a replay of what could have been done differently, and, most certainly, feelings of regret and sadness for what cannot be retrieved.

In total contrast, there is a time when we actually want something to be lost in the sea... our mistakes and, most definitely, our sins. Thankfully, as Christians, we serve a loving and forgiving God who gives us the opportunity to repent for our wrongdoings.

> *"You will again have compassion on us; you will tread our sins underfoot and hurl all our iniquities into the depths of the sea"*
>
> (MICAH 7:19 NIV)

Rest, knowing that when you sincerely asked the Lord for forgiveness of any wrong you have done, He gave it to you. Period.

Scripture:

> "If we claim to be without sin, we deceive ourselves and the truth is not in us. If we confess our sins, he is faithful and just and will forgive us our sins and purify us from all unrighteousness."
>
> (1 JOHN 1:8–9 NIV)

CHAPTER 28

SURFING

A re you a surfer? Have you ever tried to surf? Have you ever watched a person surf? How much of the act of surfing is actually controlled by the surfer, and how much is controlled by the wave? There is what looks to be amazing control over the board and over each surfer's body posture. As graceful and in-control as surfers seem, they often fall. What is the first thing a surfer does when he or she falls into the ocean? He or she gets up!

The daily happenings of life can easily be compared to the waves in the ocean. No two waves are exactly alike and no two days in life are exactly alike. There are great days and great waves to ride; there are bad days where we feel we have failed and bad waves that no surfer should ever attempt. There are long boards, short boards, fiberglass boards, and soft boards. Also, in addition to the board, other pieces of equipment are key as well. A wetsuit is essential and keeps a surfer's body warm in the cold water. Applying wax to your surfboard gives better balance overall by allowing your feet to grip the board better! And, making sure you have a tethered leash when in the water keeps you connected to the board for the times you fall ... because as we know, in surfing you *will* fall. With all of your gear in place, the next step is to practice, practice, and practice some more. Being guided by an experienced surfer is best, and being willing to give it your all when learning is key. All of these factors together lead you to success as a surfer.

As Christians, we must make sure we are properly outfitted for the waves of change, hardship, unique days and situations that come our way! We must be sure we are equipped with the right gear to handle it correctly.

> "*Therefore put on the full armor of God, so that when the day of evil comes, you may be able to stand your ground, and after you have done everything, to stand. Stand firm then, with the belt of truth buckled around your waist, with the breastplate of righteousness in place, and with*

your feet fitted with the readiness that comes from the gospel of peace. In addition to all this, take up the shield of faith, with which you can extinguish all the flaming arrows of the evil one. Take the helmet of salvation and the sword of the Spirit, which is the word of God. And pray in the Spirit on all occasions with all kinds of prayers and requests. With this in mind, be alert and always keep on praying for all the Lord's people."

(EPHESIANS 6: 13–18 NIV)

Again, what is the first thing a surfer does when he or she (wipes out) falls into the ocean? He or she immediately gets up. In life the Lord ultimately fights our battles, but he does equip us to walk through this journey of life. Make sure you are tethered to God's Word at all times. When you feel like you have been wiped out by a huge wave, look to the Lord and immediately get back up.

Scripture:

"For though the righteous fall seven times, they rise again, but the wicked stumble when calamity strikes."

(PROVERBS 24:16 NIV)

CHAPTER 29

THE PIER

The pier is used by many people as a place to take a relaxing stroll and take in the view. From the pier, the view is typically water in the front, water to the left, and water to the right. When standing seemingly on top of the depths of the sea, the magnitude of God's handiwork is all around! The pier is an easy and ideal place to stand in awe and stand in thanksgiving for all that God has done. It is a great place to reflect and give heartfelt thanks about the many trials and tribulations God has helped us endure, and it is a great place to thank God for the sunny days we already have had and continue to experience.

The next time you walk out on the pier, look at the view differently. Look at it from the perspective that God had when he looked at the creations from His hands.

> *"And God said, Let the waters under the heaven be gathered together unto one place, and let the dry land appear: and it was so. And God called the dry land Earth; and the gathering together of the waters called the Seas: and God saw that it was good."*
>
> (GENESIS 1:9–10 KJV)

The view over the ocean is a small sampling of the endless beauty, peace, and pure tranquility promised in Heaven. The pier is an exceptional place to stand in great expectation of what God will continue to do in each of our lives as Christians here on Earth, and even greater still, in Heaven. *"We wait in hope for the Lord; he is our help and our shield."* (Psalm 33:20 NIV) He is most certainly good.

Scripture:

> "Sing joyfully to the Lord, you righteous;
> it is fitting for the upright to praise him.
> Praise the Lord with the harp;
> make music to him on the ten-stringed lyre.

Sing to him a new song;
play skillfully, and shout for joy.

For the word of the Lord is right and true;
he is faithful in all he does.
The Lord loves righteousness and justice;
the earth is full of his unfailing love.

By the word of the Lord the heavens were made,
their starry host by the breath of his mouth.
He gathers the waters of the sea into jars;
he puts the deep into storehouses.
Let all the earth fear the Lord;
let all the people of the world revere him.
For he spoke, and it came to be;
he commanded, and it stood firm.

The Lord foils the plans of the nations;
he thwarts the purposes of the peoples.
But the plans of the Lord stand firm forever,
the purposes of his heart through all generations.

Blessed is the nation whose God is the Lord,
the people he chose for his inheritance.
From heaven the Lord looks down
and sees all mankind;
from his dwelling place he watches
all who live on earth—
he who forms the hearts of all,
who considers everything they do.

No king is saved by the size of his army;
no warrior escapes by his great strength.
A horse is a vain hope for deliverance;
despite all its great strength it cannot save.
But the eyes of the Lord are on those who fear him,
on those whose hope is in his unfailing love,
to deliver them from death
and keep them alive in famine.

We wait in hope for the Lord;
he is our help and our shield.
In him our hearts rejoice,
for we trust in his holy name.
May your unfailing love be with us, Lord,
even as we put our hope in you."

(PSALM 33 NIV)

CHAPTER 30

SHARING

How many pictures from the beach have you shared with others? Pictures of family lounging in a beach chair or lying on a towel in the sand? How about pictures of family members posing as the ocean waves lap around their ankles, or one of my favorites—pictures of family with the vastness of the ocean as the backdrop? There are always numerous nautical-themed photographic opportunities to capture and share from beach vacations. It is simple and easy to share your experiences with others once you get home. Just pull out your mobile phone, scroll through the images, and share. What happens when you share the pictures? Others see and sense the joy and excitement you felt from your trip. It makes them want to go as well. Right?

There is something else you can just as easily share. It is your love of Christ! As Christians, sharing our life story can be the same as sharing those fun beach vacation photos! There are numerous life opportunities captured in our past that can be shared as ways the love of Christ has impacted our daily lives. There are trials and challenges we have endured and victoriously come through, only by God's grace. Then there are the many blessings in life that again are simply by God's grace and His favor. What has God done for you? What is your testimony? What in your life do you know was the handiwork of our loving Savior? Share those stories and watch others sense the joy and excitement you feel. Scripture tells us to *"declare his glory among the nations, his marvelous deeds among all peoples."* (Psalm 96:3 NIV) Let us strive daily to reflect and share the wonderful love of Christ!

Scripture:
> "And I saw another angel fly in the midst of heaven, having the everlasting gospel to preach unto them that dwell on the earth, and to every nation, and kindred, and tongue, and people, saying with a loud voice, Fear God, and give glory to him; for the hour of his judgment is come: and worship him that made heaven, and earth, and the sea, and the fountains of waters."
>
> (REVELATION 14:6–7 KJV)

About the Author

April F. Cooper is a Christian wife, a mother to four children, and a daily grace recipient. With two master's degrees and also a graduate certificate in pastoral counseling, April tries to place encouraging others at the forefront of her life. Professionally, her career as an educator spans many years. Additionally, she is also the founder of a small nonprofit organization called "Lavender, Lilac and Lilies" that gives free floral arrangements, floral wreaths, plants, and small gifts as encouragement to those celebrating birthdays and milestones while living in shelters, senior centers, group homes, etc.

April's free time is typically spent with her family, planning dates with her husband, writing, dabbling in photography, or passionately continuing to learn American Sign Language. She firmly believes this book is a testament to what can happen when you wait on the Lord for direction. Each devotion in this book was a gift from God that April believes she was privileged to write.

To learn more about *Lavender, Lilac and Lilies*, please visit: gardeninspiration.org.